AUSTIN
TEXAS

A PHOTOGRAPHIC PORTRAIT

Photography by Rob Greebon

Narrative by Reagan O'Hare

TWIN LIGHTS PUBLISHERS | ROCKPORT, MASSACHUSETTS

Copyright © 2020 by
Twin Lights Publishers, Inc.

All rights reserved. No part of this book may be reproduced in any form without written permission of the copyright owners. All images in this book have been reproduced with the knowledge and prior consent of the artists concerned and no responsibility is accepted by producer, publisher, or printer for any infringement of copyright or otherwise, arising from the contents of this publication. Every effort has been made to ensure that credits accurately comply with information supplied.

First published in the
United States of America by:

Twin Lights Publishers, Inc.
Rockport, Massachusetts 01966
Telephone: (978) 546-7398
www.twinlightspub.com

ISBN: 978-1-934907-66-5

10 9 8 7 6 5 4 3 2 1

(opposite)
James D. Pfluger Pedestrian Bridge
Lady Bird Lake

(frontispiece)
State Capitol at Sunrise

(jacket front)
State Capitol

(jacket back)
Percy V. Pennybacker, Jr. Bridge,
Bullock Texas State History Museum

Images on pages 53 and 54 provided by Lady Bird Johnson Wildflower Center.

Images on pages 52 and 55 provided by the University of Texas.

Book design by:
SYP Design & Production, Inc.
www.sypdesign.com

Printed in China

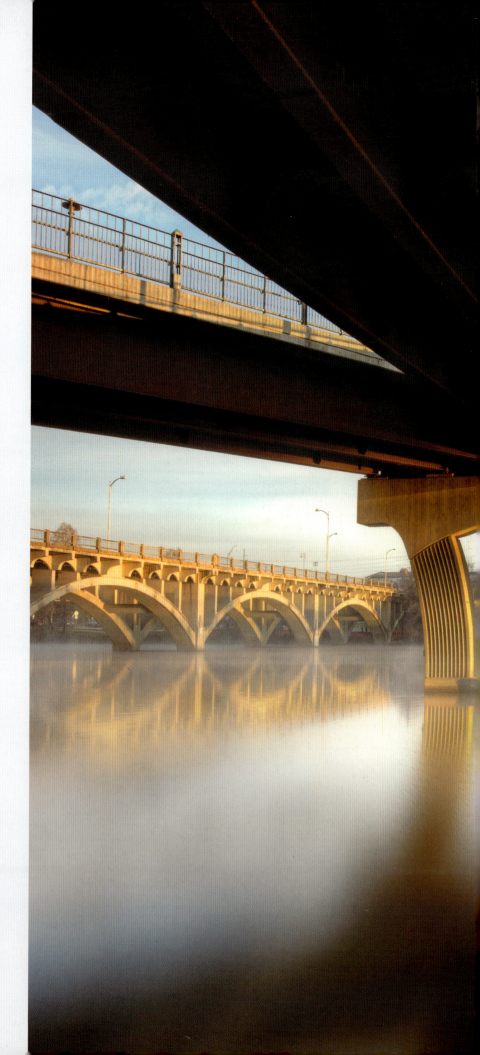

Along a bend in the Colorado River and nestled in the heart of Texas, is the city where "weird" grows. Austin, known for its colorful murals, its love affair with food trucks, and its dedication to just having fun, has an international reputation for being weird, wacky, and eccentric. On one corner, people gather to see a million bats emerge from the Congress Street Bridge while the sun sets, casting a glow onto the city. Nearby, visitors can't help but stop and take a selfie with the *Greetings from Austin* mural. At Maria's Taco Xpress, a giant sculpture of its owner tops its roof and beckons passersby to "come on in." At Laguna Gloria, a 33-foot-tall aluminum figure greets visitors next to a crying bunny fountain. "Keep Austin Weird," a slogan inspired by Red Wassenich in 2000, was adopted by the Austin Independent Business Alliance, and it stuck. In Austin, weird is the expected.

The city of "weird" is also known as the "live music capital of the world." With more than 200 music venues and buskers along many of its streets, music is engraved in the city's hill country-soul vibe. Legends like Willie Nelson, Janis Joplin, Bob Schneider, Stevie Ray Vaughan, Roky Erickson, and The Resentments, to name only a few, have made Austin musically famous. Along with talent, Austin is the music home for the internationally recognized South by Southwest and Austin City Limits music festivals. And beyond the larger venues, there are historically celebrated more-intimate venues.

But Austin is more than weird or a live music destination. Ranked as one of the fittest cities in the nation, Austin has over 300 days of sunshine a year and is a mecca for the outdoor enthusiast. The outdoors is celebrated with a kite festival, a hike and bike trail that meanders around both sides of Lady Bird Lake, and a bridge strictly dedicated to pedestrians and cyclists. And when summertime temperatures become unbearable, residents head to a 900-foot-long, spring-fed pool, waterfalls, or an emerald-green grotto. Whether it's hiking, biking, swimming, or exploring, in Austin, the possibilities are endless.

Within this central Texas space, there are places to hide, places to gaze, places to explore, and places to just be. Like that distinctive magic moment in a song when all the strings and harmonies fall into place, Austin will draw you in. Through photographer Rob Greebon's alluring images, you will see how Austin truly captures the heart of Texas.

Texas State Capitol *(opposite)*

The 1888 Texas State Capitol building is an impressive example of Renaissance Revival style, echoing the public structures of 15th- and 16th-century Italy. It is constructed of sunset red granite and stands 14 feet taller than the U.S. Capitol Building in Washington, DC. Its impressive dome, columns, and distinctive hue form its principal features.

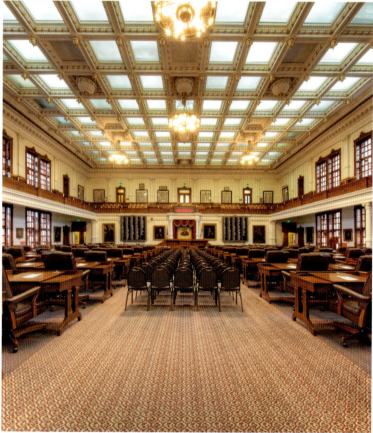

Texas State Capitol *(above)*

The central interior of the Texas State Capitol showcases an open rotunda and interior dome, which rises 266 feet from the floor. The word "Texas" surrounds an eight-foot-wide, sheet-metal star. The walls of this impressive rotunda are adorned with portraits of Texas's former governors.

House of Representatives *(left)*

The House of Representatives' room is the largest room within the Texas State Capitol building. It was restored to its original architectural details of 1909 and features oak paneling, desks, and leather chairs that are embossed with the Texas seal. Two beautifully crafted brass chandeliers hang from the ceiling.

Great Walk *(above)*

The Great Walk, a checkerboard pathway leading to the front steps of the capitol building from Congress Avenue, offers parallel rows of shade trees, lush grass, ornamental lights, and benches. The capitol's sunset red granite glows on a cool autumn morning.

Texas Capitol Visitors Center *(right)*

Located in the 1857 Land Office Building on the grounds of the capitol complex, the Capitol Visitors Center hosts a collection of interactive exhibits and films as well as a collection of historical artifacts about the history of Texas and the capitol. Daily guided tours are offered.

Congress Avenue

With six lanes and lined with trees, Congress Avenue cuts through the middle of Austin and leads straight to the Texas State Capitol. It is the city's most prominent street, where trolley cars operated on the avenue until 1940. Today, it offers a colorful view of the capitol in the early morning.

Texas State Capitol

Surrounded by 22 acres, the Texas State Capitol's park-like setting is located on a hilltop overlooking downtown Austin. A 1995-1996 restoration of the South Grounds returned the surroundings to its 1888-1915 appearance. Today the grounds are an inviting, open space.

Texas Pioneer Woman (top)

Sculpted to celebrate the spirit and heroism of the pioneer women of early Texas, Texas Pioneer Woman, a bronze figure of a young woman cradling her baby in one arm, was created by Linda Sioux Henley and erected in 1998 on the grounds of the capitol. This life-size figure stands atop a sunset red granite pedestal.

Tejano Monument (bottom)

Designed by Armando Hinojosa, Tejano Monument was erected in 2012. It celebrates the origin of Texas by Spanish and Mexican explorers and settlers. The base includes statues that historically depict the *Tejano* (Texan) settlement and include a Spanish explorer, a cowboy on his mustang, longhorn cattle, and a family of settlers.

Trail of Trees

Beginning at the State Seal outside the south entrance to the Texas State Capitol building, *Trail of Trees* is a guide that informs visitors about the 25 varieties of trees that are planted on the historic capitol grounds. The grounds feature hundreds of trees, monuments, and fountains.

Texas Children Monument
(above and opposite)

Tribute to Texas Schoolchildren is a life-sized bronze depicting children on a field trip to the Texas State Capitol. Erected in 1998 and designed by Lawrence Ludtke, it "pays tribute to the citizens who will shape the future of Texas." The project was funded by children from more than 600 Texas schools.

Korean War Veterans Memorial *(above)*

Located on the capitol grounds, the Korean War Veterans Memorial honors the 289,000 Texans who served in the war. Created by Edward L. Hankey in 1999, a bronze eagle sits atop a granite pedestal. Etched in the base are the names of the 1,723 soldiers missing or killed in action.

Pearl Harbor Monument *(left)*

Designed by Scott Field and erected in 1989, the Pearl Harbor Monument honors the Texas men and women who were present on the island of Oahu when Japanese attacked Pearl Harbor in 1941. Located on the capitol grounds, the memorial's base is made of sunset red granite and marble.

Volunteer Fireman Monument (left)

The original stone memorial to volunteer firefighters was replaced around 1905 by this bronze sculpture by J. Segesman. The monument depicts a fireman carrying a child and a lantern. The granite base and a ring of granite pillars list the names of Texan volunteer firefighters who lost their lives fighting fires.

Spanish War Veteran Monument (right)

This Spanish American War Monument, the *Hiker*, was sculpted by Theo Alice Ruggles Kitson and is one of more than 50 *Hiker* statues placed throughout the United States. During the Spanish War, Americans referred to themselves as "hikers." Erected in 1951, it honors the memory of veterans of the war.

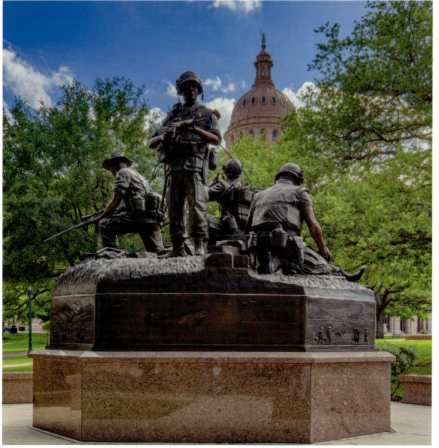

Texas Peace Officers' Memorial *(above)*

The Texas Peace Officers' Memorial, designed by Linda Johnson, is a polished granite obelisk with adjoining walls on a base with the Texas Lone Star. Located on the capitol grounds, the memorial's walls are inscribed with the names of the officers who have lost their lives in the line of duty since 1823.

Vietnam Veterans Monument *(left)*

The Vietnam Veterans Monument was designed by Duke Sundt and sculpted by Clint Howard and Jake Jakovich. Dedicated in 2014, it honors the Texans who died or went missing during the war, as well as those who served. Entombed are 3,417 hand-embossed dog tags for each of the Texans who died in service.

World War II Memorial *(above)*

This 2007 World War II Memorial is a replica of the Texas pillar at the WW II Memorial in Washington, DC. It honors the Texans who served in World War II, the more than 22,000 who died during the war, and the millions who supported the war effort from home.

World War I Monument *(right)*

Erected in 1961 by the Veterans of Foreign Wars, this World War I Monument commemorates the more than 190,000 Texas veterans of the First World War. Located on the grounds of the State Capitol, near the Texas Supreme Court building, the monument is made from polished sunset red granite.

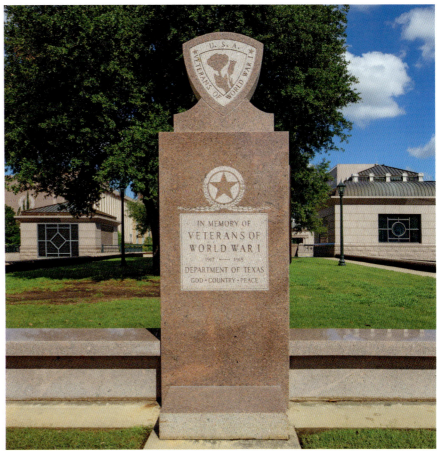

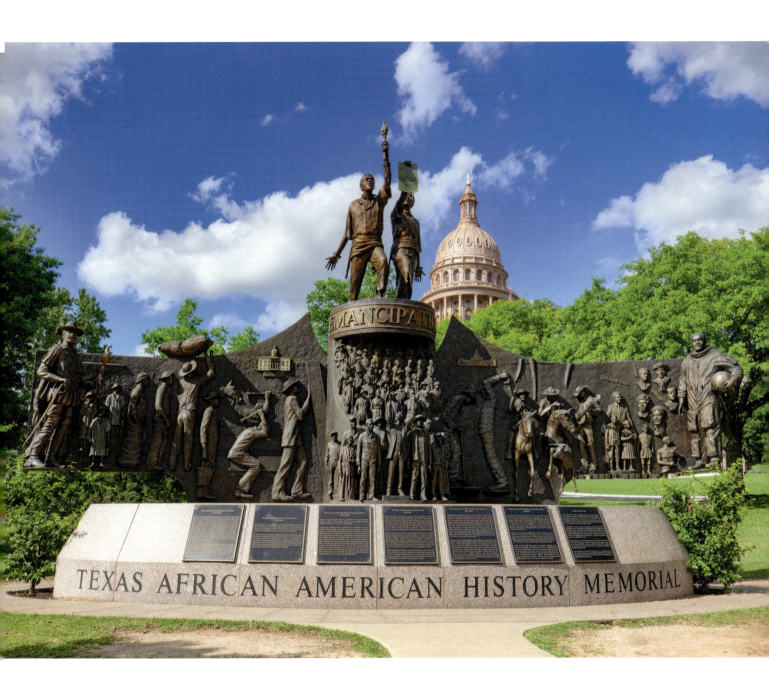

Statue of Liberty *(opposite top)*

Donated in 1951 by the Boy Scouts of America, this Statue of Liberty replica was moved to its current location during the 1990s grounds restoration. At that time, a time capsule was discovered, which was relocated to the Boy Scout's base near Bastrop and will be opened in 2076.

Ten Commandments *(opposite bottom)*

Presented by the Fraternal Order of Eagles in 1961, the Ten Commandments Monument shares the biblical commandments of moral code. Standing 6 feet tall, 3 feet wide, and in the traditional shape of biblical stones, it is located on the grounds of the capitol.

The Texas African American History Memorial *(above)*

The Texas African American History Memorial, erected in 2016, honors the African American celebration of freedom on June 19, 1895, and traces their history from the 1500s to present. The bronze and granite sculpture by Ed Dwight salutes leaders Hendrick Arnold and Barbara Jordan.

Austin City Hall *(top and bottom)*

Designed in 2004 by Antoine Predock Architects, City Hall reflects the warm informality of the city. Incorporating limestone and a nonsymmetrical shape, more than 66,000 square feet of cooper wraps around the top half of the building and is expected to last two-three times longer than conventional materials.

Austin City Hall *(opposite)*

Made 70% of recycled materials and adorned with 1,500 plants, City Hall is a gathering place for community collaboration. *The People's Gallery* exhibition spans the first three floors of the building and showcases artwork from local and regional artists. The exhibition is designed to reflect the excellence and cultural diversity of the city.

Frost Bank Tower *(opposite and top)*

One of Austin's most recognizable architectural icons is Frost Bank Tower. It stands 515 feet tall with 33 floors and is the fourth largest building in Austin. The tower was completed in 2004 with a blue, low-emissivity glass coating, seen in only a few skyscrapers across the United States.

View from the Austonian *(bottom)*

The award-winning Austonian is the tallest residential building in Texas. Acclaimed as a low-water conservation establishment with high-quality amenities, The Austonian is located within walking distance of nearly 100 restaurants, shops, and entertainment facilities.

James D. Pfluger Pedestrian Bridge
(above and opposite top)

The James D. Pfluger Bridge was named after an influential Austin architect. Opened in 2001, it runs parallel to the original Lamar Bridge and allows bikers and pedestrians to view the city and lake, 400 feet below. Not far from the city's music hub, it's popular for an easy evening stroll.

Austin from Above *(bottom)*

Austin is booming, and its skyline is continually changing, yet the feeling of creativity and innovation remain. Skyline views are best seen from the Long Center, Zilker Park, the 360 Bridge, and the Pfluger Bridge. This view of the Texas State Capitol is looking down at the Congress Avenue Bridge.

Lone Star Riverboat
(above and left)

Lone Star Riverboat cruises are a great way to view Lady Bird Lake, to capture views of the city, and to get up close to the Congress Street Bridge. These electric, environment-friendly boats and narrated tours are available during the day, by moonlight, or specifically for bat flight gazing.

Austin Skyline *(top and bottom)*

Austin's skyline is remarkable during evening hours. Reflected in the still water of Lady Bird Lake, the city is bustling with music, visitors, and many new-to-Austin recruits. The Austonian, currently the tallest building in the city, rises above the iconic Frost Tower.

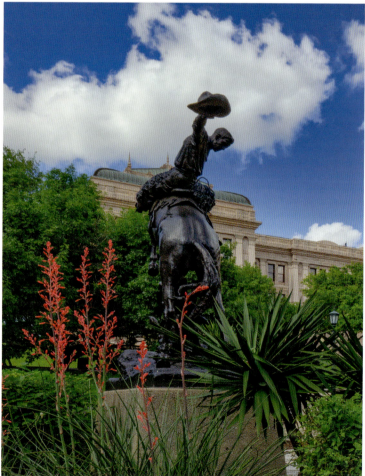

Texas Cowboy Monument *(above and left)*

The Texas Cowboy Monument by Constance Whitney Warren was sculpted in 1921 and donated to the city in 1925, where it was installed on the Texas State Capitol grounds. Inspired by animals, horses, and frontier life, Warren was one of the first female sculptors to produce large bronze sculptures in the early 20th century.

Boardwalk

Constructed in 2014, this mile-long boardwalk on Lady Bird Lake completed the 10-mile loop of the Ann and Roy Butler Hike-and-Bike Trail. The boardwalk is Austin's most popular and recognized recreational area and is a favorite spot for sunset walks, jogging, bicycling, and skyline gazing.

Bats over Congress Avenue

(above and opposite)

Sunset bat gazing draws crowds from March through November when roughly 1.5 million Mexican free-tailed bats emerge from beneath the Congress Avenue Bridge to devour 20,000 lbs. of insects. The first cloud of bats usually emerge right after sunset and return about 30 minutes before sunrise.

Percy V. Pennybacker, Jr. Bridge
(pages 32–33)

A short hike from the road to this overlook, on the right, is a great place for a picnic and to enjoy stunning views of the Pennybacker Bridge, Lake Austin, and the Austin skyline. It is known locally as the 360 Bridge because it connects the northern and southern sections of the Loop 360 Highway.

Percy V. Pennybacker, Jr. Bridge
(above and opposite)

Opened in 1982, the Pennybacker Bridge is 1,150 feet long and is comprised of 600 tons of steel and 3,400 tons of concrete. Named after Percy Pennybacker, Jr., a bridge designer and a pioneer in welded structure technology, the bridge's weathered rust finish blends in with the surrounding hills.

Lamar Bridge Sculler *(pages 36–37)*

Just after sunrise, a sculler rows through the calm waters of Lady Bird Lake beneath the Lamar Boulevard Bridge. Often seen in the early morning hours, rowers and scullers launch from several facilities along the river where boat and equipment rentals are available as well as introductory lessons.

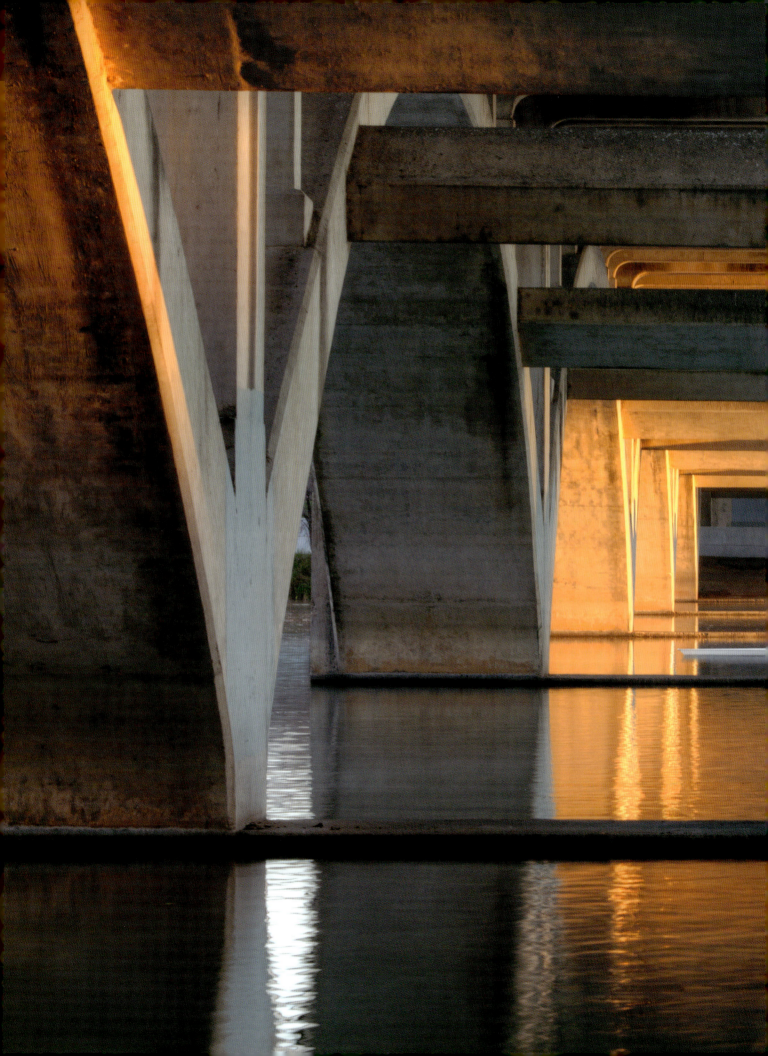

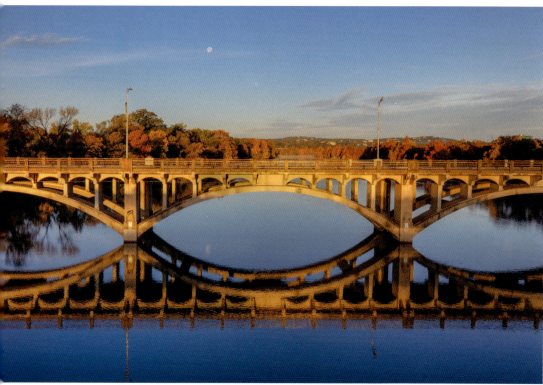

View from Mount Bonnell (top)

Mount Bonnell is a Texas Historic Landmark with great views of the Colorado River, the 360 Bridge, and downtown Austin. Located at Covert Park, 102 stairs from the main trailhead lead visitors to the summit of Mount Bonnell—the highest spot in Austin at 775 feet.

Lamar Boulevard Bridge (bottom)

Crossing over the Colorado River, the Lamar Boulevard Bridge opened in 1942 and was named an Austin Landmark in 1993. Made of reinforced concreted and spanning 659 feet, it features six open arches. The bridge was constructed without sidewalks or bicycle lanes, thus leading to the building of the Pfluger Pedestrian Bridge.

Full Moon over Austin

A full moon over Austin is a glorious foreshadowing of adventurous evenings. By day, the city is a typical place of business, but in the evenings, Austin's city streets come to life with live music, entertainment, bat-gazing, and moonlight boat tours.

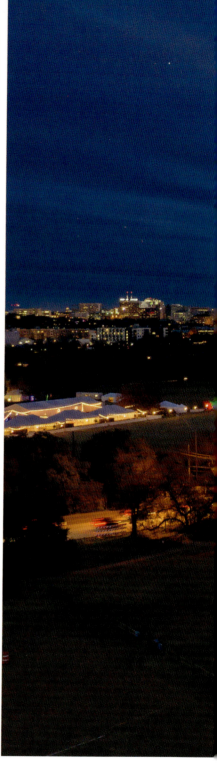

Liz Carpenter Fountain
(top and bottom)

Named after Lady Bird Johnson's writer and former press secretary, the Liz Carpenter Fountain at Butler Park enchants children of all ages. A magical spot to cool off during warm summer days and nights, the fountain transforms into a colorful light show each evening from sunset to 9:45 PM.

Zilker Tree at Night

The Austin Trail of Lights Celebration began in 1965 and is Austin's second-largest event. Held at Zilker Park and with more than two million lights, the event attracts families of all ages. Food trucks, music, and events are an enjoyable way to celebrate the holiday season.

Barton Springs Pool *(top and bottom)*

Barton Springs Pool, Austin's favorite swimming hole, attracts nearly 800,000 visitors annually. This spring-fed pool was constructed in the 1920s and is located on the grounds of Zilker Park. Its clear, 68- to 70-degree water and spacious grassy area is the perfect place to spend the day swimming or sunbathing.

Barton Springs Pool

A refreshing way to escape the summer heat, the 900-foot-long Barton Springs Pool flows into Barton Creek and then to Lady Bird Lake. Efforts to keep the springs safe from development are lead by the Save Our Springs Alliance, an organization dedicated to the preservation of this natural treasure.

Barton Springs *(top and bottom)*

The Edwards Aquifer spills an average of 27 million gallons of water a day into Barton Springs. Located in Zilker Park, Barton Springs' Main Spring feeds Barton Springs Pool. A favorite destination for Austinites, the pool is home to salamanders, turtles, eels, crawfish, and more.

Barton Creek Greenbelt (above)

Barton Creek Greenbelt contains more than 12 miles of gorgeous trails and is considered one of the top hiking trails in Texas. With multiple entry points and just five miles from downtown Austin, it attracts bikers, rock climbers, hikers, and swimmers. Twin Falls is a cherished swimming hole within the greenbelt.

Sculpture Falls (pages 46–47)

Located just 1.25 miles from Twin Falls, water from Sculpture Falls cascades over naturally eroded limestone and leads to a 70-degree pool. Years of water flowing over this limestone ledge have carved beautiful patterns into the rock. The perfect spot for cooling off, it attracts both Austinites and visitors alike.

Umlauf Sculpture Garden & Museum

Acclaimed artist Charles Umlauf and his wife Angeline donated their home, studio, and numerous sculptures to the city of Austin in 1985. In 1991 a museum was built to celebrate his work. Located within Zilker Park, numerous artworks are on display, including *Mother and Child* and *Father and Son*.

Umlauf Garden Interior *(top)*

This open-air museum and garden is home to the largest collection of Umlauf's work as well as other contemporary sculptors. Light captures the glow of the garden and interior architectural details. Built with private funds, it is a popular location for elegant weddings, private parties, and other events.

Umlauf Garden *(bottom)*

Art and landscape complement each other in this serene garden. Designed as a shady spot to escape Austin's summer hear, the garden is a natural setting to enjoy nature and art. The arbor of trees allows visitors to comfortably stroll the garden and linger near each work of art.

Mother and Child *(above)*

Interested in carving and forming figures from an early age, Charles Umlauf received his first commission of a full-sized lion at the age of eleven. Born in Michigan, he moved his family to Austin, where he taught for 40 years at the University of Texas. *Mother and Child* was sculpted in 1960.

Seated Bather *(left)*

Casually standing and restfully reclining bathers were a common theme for American sculptor Charles Umlauf in 1958. *Seated Bather* was cast in bronze in 1965. An enlarged version of it is located nearby, within the Umlauf Sculpture Garden. The grounds feature gravel paths, native plants, a waterfall, and ponds.

Icarus (left)

In Greek mythology, Daedalus made his son wings out of feathers and wax to escape the island of Crete. Ignoring his father's warning, Icarus flew to close to the sun and fell into the sea when his wings melted. Charles Umlauf captures the essence of this mythological tale in his bronze sculpture, *Icarus*.

The Kiss (right)

Inspired by French sculptor Auguste Rodin's *Kiss*, Charles Umlauf's 1970 bronze *The Kiss* is located on a small island in the center of one of two ponds. *The Kiss* was prominently placed near a space designed for wedding ceremonies. The garden's six acres are defined by a large oval path surrounding a "Y."

University of Texas *(opposite)*

The University of Texas at Austin is the education hub of Austin. Founded in 1883, today it represents at least 124 countries and students from all 50 states. The university includes nine academic schools and six health institutions with more than 50,000 students and 3,000 faculty members.

Lady Bird Johson Wildflower Center *(above)*

Home to 900 species of native plants, 148 bird species, and 284 acres of cultivated gardens, the current campus opened in 1995 and today hosts nearly 200,000 guests annually. With 1,800 insect species and 93 varieties of butterflies, it is internationally recognized for plant conservation and education.

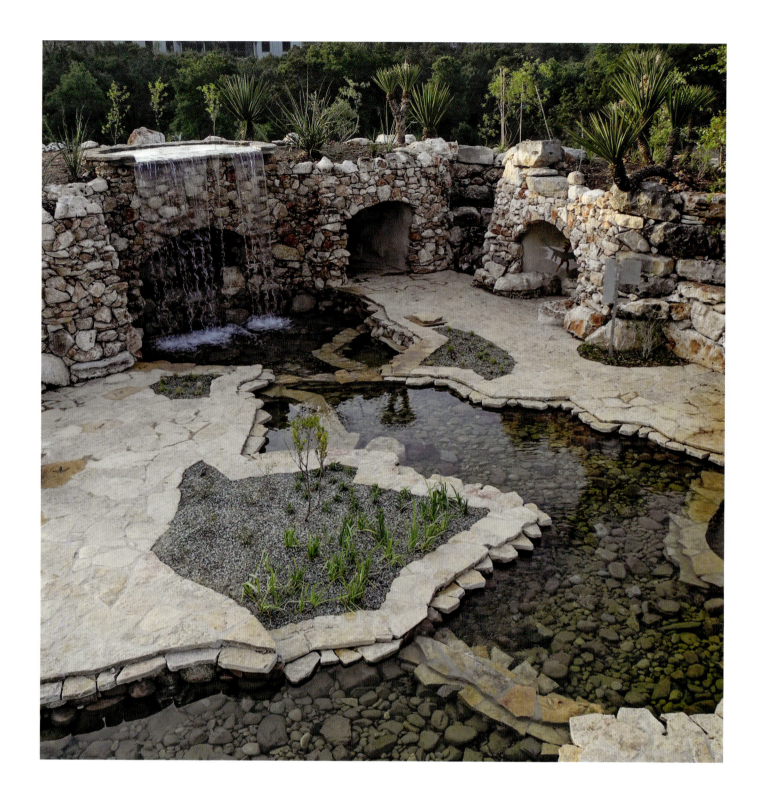

Luci and Ian Family Garden *(above)*

Opened in 2014 in the Lady Bird Johnson Wildflower Center, the 4.5-acre Luci and Ian Family Garden offers interactive and educational features made of natural materials. This grotto, with caves and a waterfall, is one of more than a dozen features that children and families enjoy.

Littlefield Fountain *(opposite top)*

Pompeo Coppini created Littlefield Fountain for the University of Texas in 1932. The sculpture is comprised of a prow of a ship, *Columbia* holding two torches, two military figures, three seahorses, and two mermen. The fountain is a popular spot for graduation photos.

Texas Memorial Museum *(opposite bottom)*

Located at the University of Texas, the Texas Memorial Museum was designed by John F. Staub with Paul Cret. Opened in 1939, it cultivates the education of natural history. Exhibits feature dinosaur fossils, a flying reptile, meteorites, a paleo lab, Texas wildlife, and more.

Austin Convention and Visitor Center
(opposite top)

The Neal Kocurek Memorial Austin Convention Center was built in 1992 and hosts half a million guests annually. Within the building is the Austin Visitor Center, where the staff shares their knowledge of Austin's history, restaurants, events, and more. The center provides brochures and free WiFi.

Contemporary Austin-Jones Center
(opposite bottom)

Celebrating modern art through education, exhibitions, and art preservation, The Contemporary, on Congress Street, is Austin's primary art museum. The center offers contemporary art within multiple street-level galleries, a large gallery on the second floor, and a rooftop deck.

Angelina Eberly Statue *(above)*

In 1842, Sam Houston attempted to move the Texas capitol from Austin to Houston. While Texas Ranges rounded up government archives, Angelina Eberly fired off the town cannon and roused its citizens to return the archives to town. Pat Oliphant's 2004 sculpture of Eberly captures the "it's-mine spirit" of Austin.

6th Street *(above and left)*

Austin's iconic 6th Street is the entertainment hub of Austin and the epicenter of the "live music capital of the world" with more live music venues per capita than anywhere else in the country. During the day, 6th Street is popular for fine dining, bakeries, and shops.

The Driskill *(opposite)*

Located on 6th Street and Brozas Street, this Romanesque-style building is one of the most historic landmarks in Austin. Constructed in 1886 by Colonel Jesse Driskill, the luxurious Driskill hotel was built as a showpiece for Austin and became the location for inaugural balls.

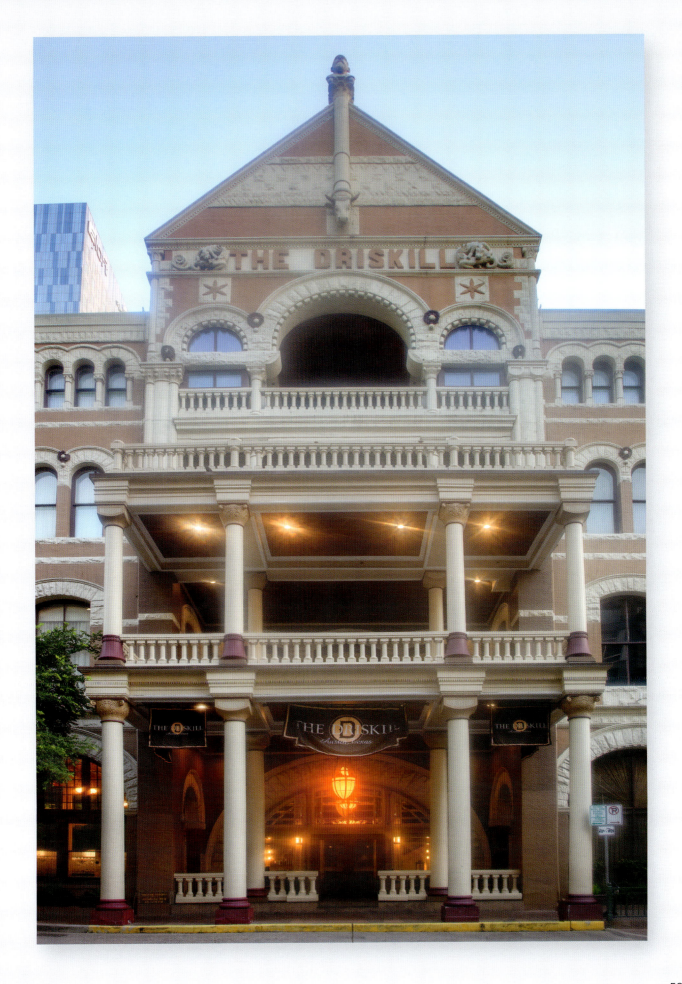

1886 Café & Bakery

A favorite bakery for many, the hotels 1886 Café & Bakery opened in 2002 on the first floor. Originally the 1886 Lunchroom, today time-honored original recipe comfort foods are served. Visitors often see a 1900s bakery truck along the outside of the café.

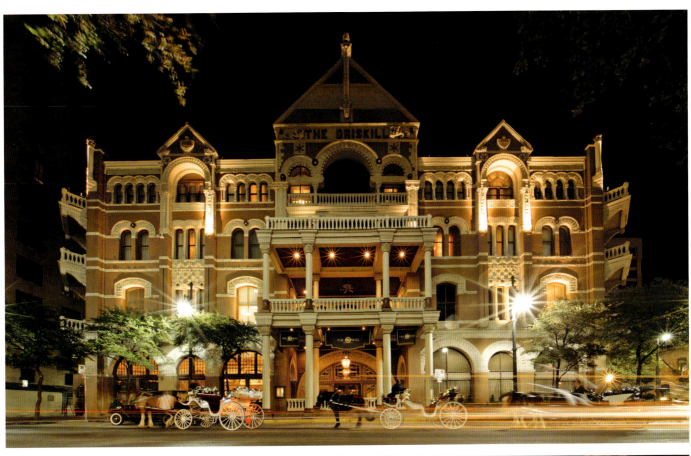

Carriage Rides *(above)*

Romantic carriage rides are an enjoyable way to experience downtown Austin. Decorated in holiday lights, The Driskill is a beautiful place for wedding receptions, second honeymoons, or a day trip to enjoy an elegant meal.

Interior Splendor *(right)*

Known for its exquisite cuisine and elegant architectural details, The Driskill features a grand lobby with gleaming marble floors and a stained-glass dome. A sweeping grand stairway, 189 historic guestrooms, an extensive collection of artworks, nightly live music, and more add to its spectacular ambiance.

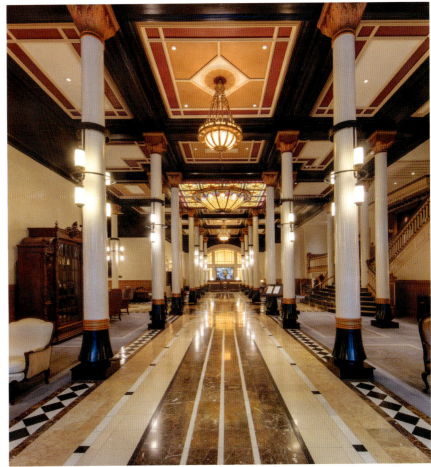

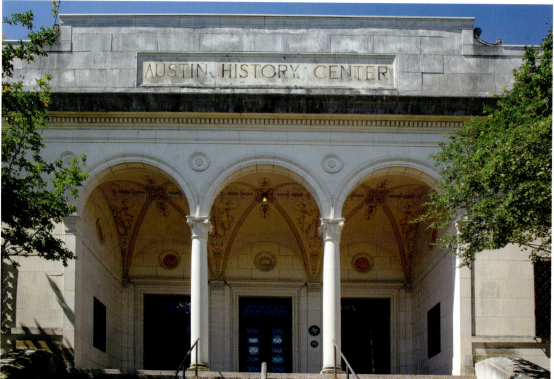

Bullock Texas State History Museum *(top and opposite)*

Home to more than 700 Texas artifacts and hundreds of first-hand stories, this treasured museum honors former Texas Lieutenant Governor Robert "Bob" Douglas Bullock. Constructed in 2001, the museum has rotating exhibits, an IMAX theater, a gift shop, educational programs, and more.

Austin History Center *(bottom)*

The local history division of the Austin Public Library, the Austin History Center is a bank of knowledge. It has over one million images from the mid-19th century to present and more than 22,000 items, including books, government documents, and unpublished reports documenting the history and current activities of Austin and Travis County.

Emma S. Barrientos Mexican American Cultural Center *(top and bottom)*

The Mexican American Cultural Center celebrates Mexican American and Latino heritage through education, research, and a variety of artistic programs. Opened in 2007 under the direction of Teodoro Gonzalez de Leon, it attracts more than 100,000 visitors annually.

Tejano Music Legends

Tejano Music Legends was sculpted by Carmen Arismendi in 2015. It celebrates the contributions of the Perez and Ramos families that were integral to the Austin music scene. Their culture and talent are exemplified in the four figures. The Perez brothers are playing the saxophone, and the Ramos brothers are engaged in song.

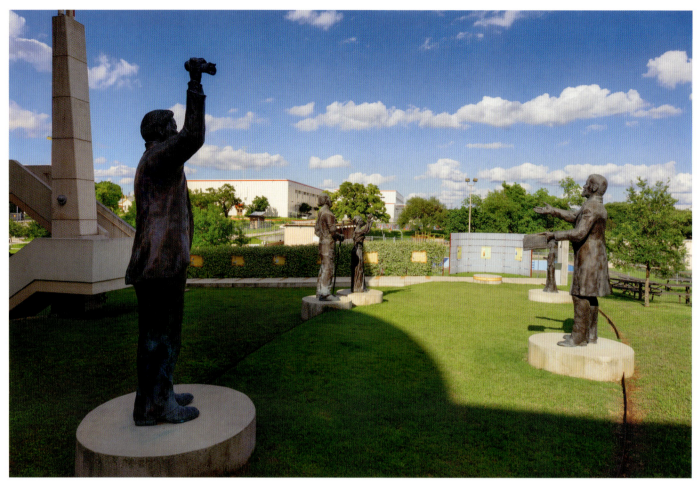

Juneteenth Memorial *(above and left)*

Located on the grounds of the George Washington Carver Museum, the Juneteenth Memorial was named after the date when the people of Texas were informed that all slaves were free. Sculpted by Eddie Dixon and Adrienne Rison Isom, the memorial includes five bronze sculptures: a lawmaker, a minister, and an enslaved couple and their daughter.

George Washington Carver Museum *(opposite top and bottom)*

Dedicated to the preservation, research, and exhibition of Austin's African American heritage, this 36,000-square-foot museum has four galleries, a 134-seat theatre, classrooms, and more. *Go Forth*, by Eddie Dixon, is a bronze sculpture of a female figure (Eternity) ushering forth a girl (Today) and a boy (Tomorrow).

Texas Military Museum
(opposite top and bottom)

Located within Camp Mabry, the museum's 45,000 square feet of military artifacts showcase the history of Texas' militia, volunteer forces, and Texas Military Forces from 1823 to present. Galleries also include the history of the Texas Air National Guard, 36th Infantry Division, and the Lost Battalion.

Texas Military Museum *(above)*

Luring military history buffs along MoPac with a peak of jet fighters and helicopters, the Texas Military Museum offers several outdoor exhibits. Armor Row, Artillery Park, and the Parade Ground are located around the museum and showcase artillery, tanks, armored personnel carriers, and more.

Texas Military Museum *(top and bottom)*

The Texas Military Museum's exhibits include the Main Gallery, Lost Battalion Gallery, Great Hall, World War II Pacific Theater, Air Guard Gallery, and the 36 Division Gallery. Among the artifacts in the Great Hall is a WWII Gratitude Train, a Sherman Tank HQ 18, and Army vehicles.

Texas Military Museum

The Great Hall at the Texas Military Museum features large artifacts that range from horse-drawn wagons to weapons used through the two world wars, the Cold War, and the War on Terror. A Schwarzlose Machine Gun and a Howitzer artillery weapon are on display as well as exhibits on the Texas National Guard.

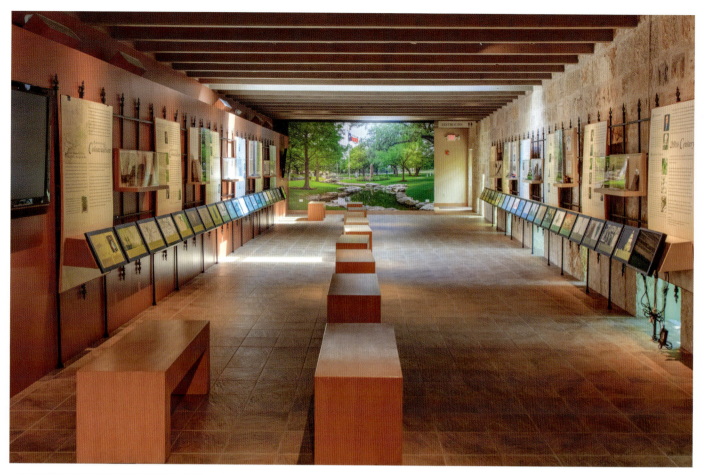

Texas State Cemetery *(above and left)*

The Texas State Cemetery is located one mile from the Texas State Capitol and is the burial place for famous Texans. Notable monuments line the grounds and include the Purple Heart Monument, which is dedicated to the brave men and women who were wounded in all of the United States' wars.

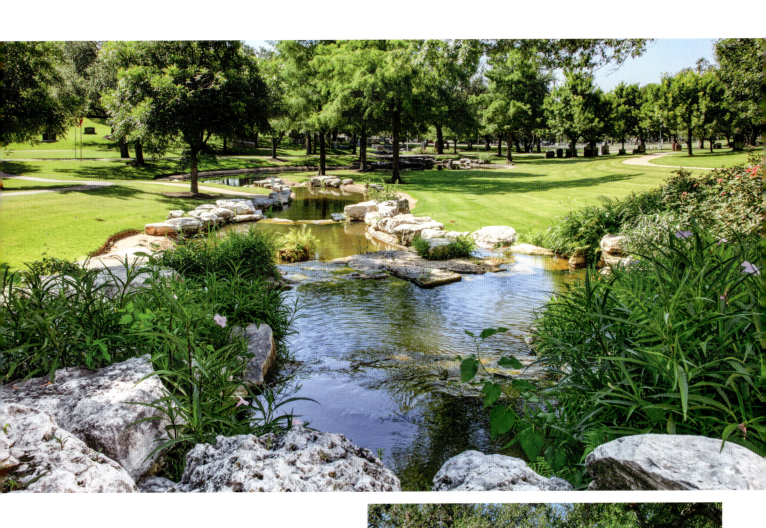

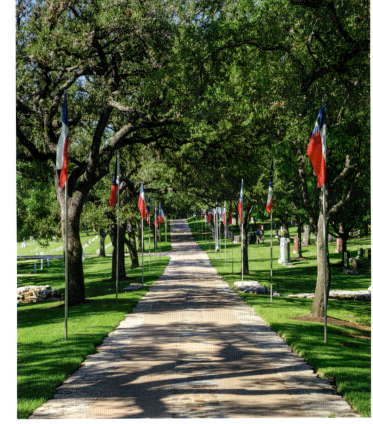

Texas State Cemetery *(above and right)*

Established in 1851, the beautifully maintained grounds of the Texas State Cemetery feature a winding brook and walkways lined with Texas flags. It's a reflective stroll where visitors learn about notable Texans who helped establish Austin. Buried here are Stephen F. Austin, General Albert Sidney Johnston, and Lieutenant Governor Bob Bullock.

The Contemporary Laguna Gloria
(above and left)

The Contemporary Austin is comprised of two locations, one being Laguna Gloria. This 14-acre site overlooks Lake Austin and features the Edward Marcus Sculpture Park, where both temporary and permanent art is installed. The *Miffy Fountain* by Dick Burna and Tom Sachs was installed in 2008.

The Contemporary Laguna Gloria
(above and right)

The former home of Clara Driscoll, this 1916 Italianate-style villa was donated to the city in 1943. Today, the museum offers exhibits by local and regional artists, events, and classes at the Art School. *Looking Up* by Tom Friedman and a cherub fountain are located on the grounds.

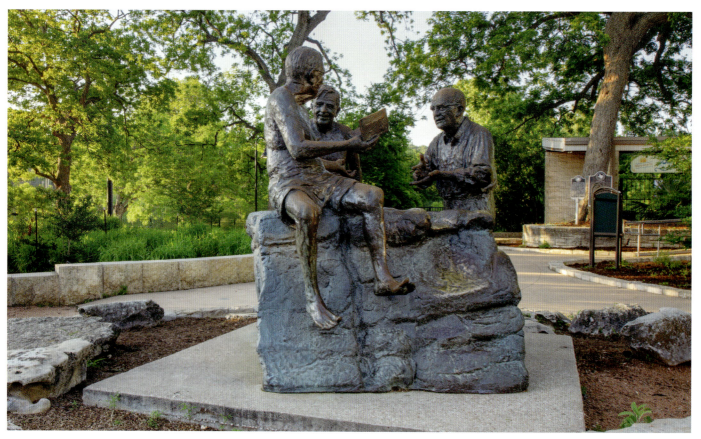

Philosophers' Rock (above)

Three prominent Austin intellects, Walter Prescott Webb, J. Frank Dobie, and Roy Bedichek, met regularly at Barton Springs Pool. *Philosophers' Rock*, by Glenna Goodacre, pays homage to friends, ideas, and the glory of nature. The sculpture was erected in 1994 and is located near the entrance to Barton Springs Pool.

Elisabet Ney Museum (left)

The Elisabet Ney Museum is the former home and studio of Elisabet Ney, a women's rights activist and contemporary artist. Ney's art, history, and legacy are featured through exhibitions, educational programs, and more. Works include 19th-century European dignitaries and life-sized works of Stephen F. Austin and Sam Houston.

Wild Basin Wilderness Preserve
(above and right)

Founded in 1974 by seven women, this preserve includes 227 acres of natural habitat, 2.5 miles of well-maintained hiking trails, and the Creative Research Center operated by St. Edwards University. Part of the Balcones Canyonlands Preserve, it offers nature tours, educational events, classroom space, and more.

Zilker Botanical Garden *(above and left)*

Known as the "Jewel in the heart of Austin," Zilker Botanical Garden is located within Zilker Park. Opened in 1969, renowned landscape architect Isamu Taniguchi spent 18 months creating a 3-acre garden. *Bridge to Walk Over the Moon* was positioned so that when the moon is high, it is reflected in the water.

Isamu Taniguchi Japanese Garden

Gardens, trails, seasonal bedding displays, a pioneer village, and more depict varied topography at Zilker Botanical Garden. A popular attraction at the Isamu Taniguchi Japanese Garden is this koi-filled pond. More than 125,000 visitors explore the gardens annually for educational events and family fun.

Zilker Botanical Garden *(above and left)*

Waterlilies, purple cornflowers, and perennial hibiscus bloom at Zilker Botanical Garden. It is comprised of the Green Garden, Cactus and Succulent Garden, Hartman Prehistoric Garden, Herb and Fragrance Garden, Isamu Taniguchi Japanese Garden, Mabel Davis Rose Garden, Doug Blachly Butterfly Trail and Garden, and the Children's Garden.

Swedish Cabin

Built circa 1838 and purchased in the 1850s by Sven Swenson, the Swedish Pioneer Cabin is considered one of the best-preserved log cabins in the U.S. The Texas Swedish Pioneers Association moved the cabin to Zilker Botanical Garden in 1965. Swenson and his uncle were responsible for aiding Swedish immigration to Texas.

Phillips-Bremond-Houston House
(above)

Serenaded by beautiful oak trees and lush green grounds, the 1855 Phillips-Bremond-Houston House was owned by Phillips, Bremond, and Houston families. Bremond Historic District, named after brothers Eugene and John Bremond, prominent members of the banking and mercantile industry, consists of 11 houses built between the 1850s to 1910.

Bremond Historic District
(left and opposite)

Home to the Texas Classroom Teachers Association, the 1886 John Bremond, Jr. House is a graceful example of Texas Victorian architecture. A cast-iron wrap-around porch, bracketed curves on the front gable, a crested mansard roof, and slate shingles make it one of the most outstanding houses in the historic district.

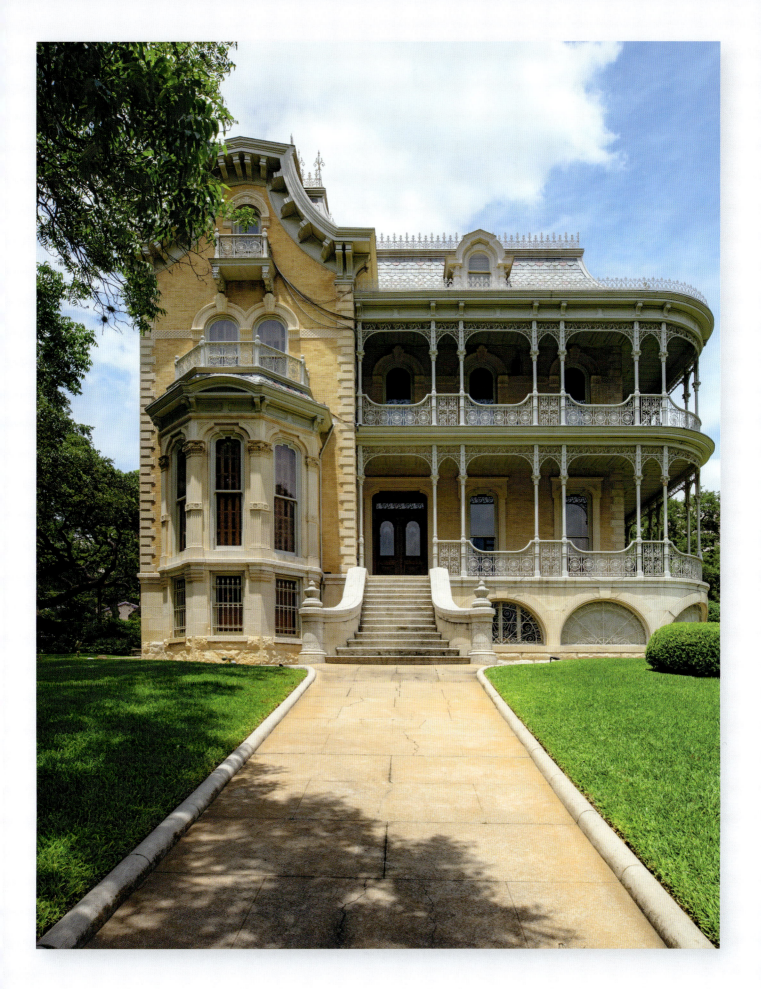

Bremond Historic District
(above and left)

The Bremond Historic District's Victorian and modest Greek Revival homes were part of Eugene Bremond's original vision of a family compound. The district was added to the National Register of Historic Places in 1970. The homes are reflective of the economic changes in the family as well as in Austin.

Neill Cochran House Museum *(above)*

The 1855 Neill-Cochran House Museum offers an authentic look at Austin life in the mid-19th through early 20th century. One of Austin's ten oldest buildings, this Greek Revival museum is furnished with historic treasures, artwork, and artifacts. The museum may also be rented for events.

O. Henry Museum *(right)*

One of the most popular short-story writers of his time, William Sydney Porter (O. Henry), lived in this house from 1893-1895 while writing for his newspaper publication *Rolling Stone*. The house was moved to its current location in 1934 and focuses on the author's Austin years and his earliest stories.

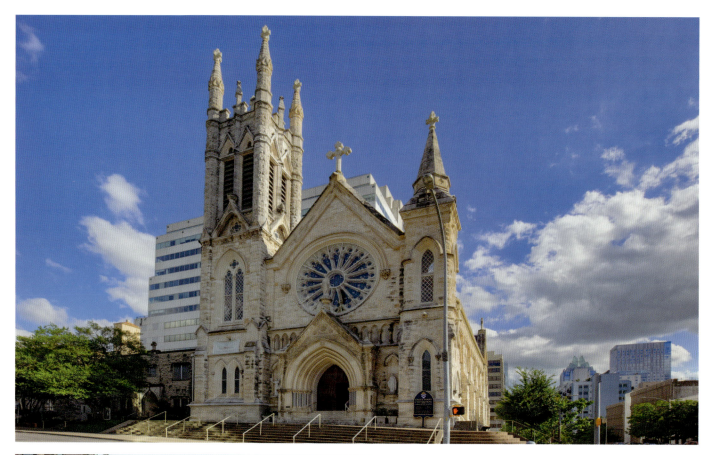

Saint Mary Cathedral *(above)*

Featuring an elegant stained-glass rose window and bell tower, St. Mary Cathedral was designed by Nicholas Clayton. The cathedral was Clayton's first independent commission, which led him to become the foremost Victorian architect in Texas. The structure was completed in 1874 and added to the National Register of Historic Places.

St. David's Episcopal Church *(left)*

One of the oldest standing buildings in Austin, St. David's Episcopal Church, laid its first cornerstone in 1853 and features 20 stained glass windows that date from 1876-1969. The church's marble alter dates from 1900, and many of the choir stalls and chairs date from the 1800s.

Governor's Mansion *(opposite)*

Home to every governor since 1856, the Governor's Mansion of Texas was designed by architect Abner Cook and features a deep veranda, floor-length windows, and wide hallways. Ten rooms in the mansion contain a collection of art, governor's mementos, and furniture, including Sam Houston's bed.

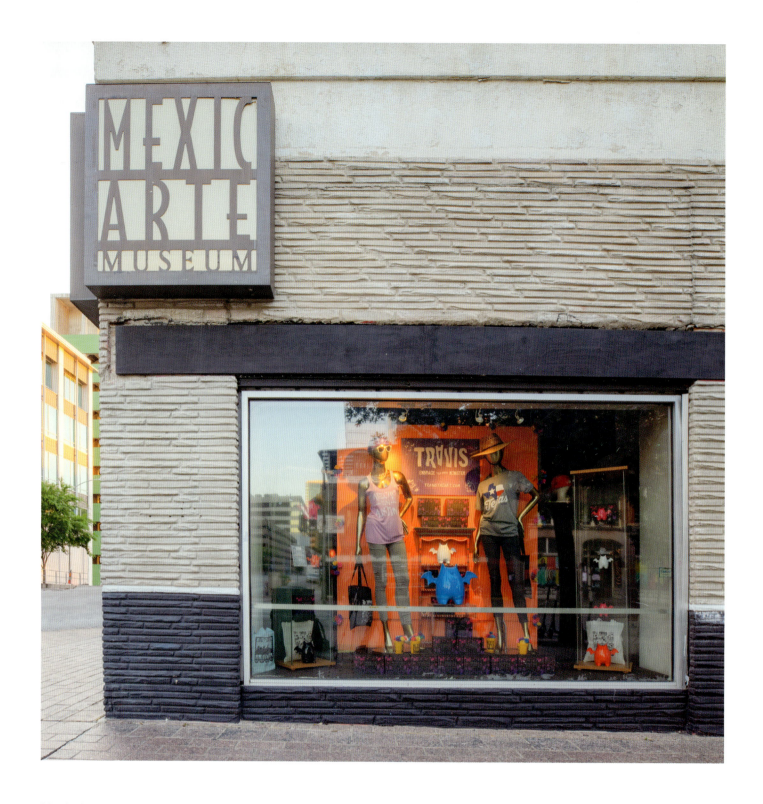

Mexic-Arte Museum

The Official Mexican and Mexican American Fine Art Museum of Texas, the Mexic-Arte Museum, was founded in 1984 by Sylvia Orozco, Sam Coronado, and Pio Pulido. Committed to the enrichment, education, and preservation of Mexican, Latin American, and Latino art, its rotating exhibits highlight traditional and contemporary art.

SoCo (above)

With magnificent views of the Texas State Capitol, South Congress, or "SoCo," is one of Austin's most popular spots for shopping, dining, dog walking, sightseeing, and enjoying live music. SoCo also offers artisan markets, food trucks, and Lucy in Disguise, a costume shop like no other.

Buskers (right)

Woodstock James, one of the many colorful buskers along SoCo, entertains visitors and locals alike. Known as the "live music capital of the world," busking is a way for musicians, dancers, mimes, and poets to have their talents seen and heard, and adds a unique layer of spice to what makes Austin weird.

Barton Springs Saloon *(above)*

Barton Springs Saloon, a popular local watering hole, is located near the Austin City Limits Music Festival sign and down the street from Austin's favorite swimming spot. The saloon is housed in a converted gas station and offers a casual atmosphere and an outdoor patio.

Old Bakery and Emporium *(left)*

Full of unique arts and crafts, the Old Bakery and Emporium is a consignment shop, visitor center, and it houses the Lundberg-Maerki Historical Collection. Built in 1874, this national landmark served as a bakery until 1936. Today, it connects with the community with special programs and events.

Mean-Eyed Cat Bar (above)

An Austin favorite known for its Do-Rite BBQ, desserts, and local and craft beers, the Mean-Eyed Cat honors Johnny Cash. Named after his 1960's tune and located in a building that was once a chainsaw repair shop, its interior is decorated with Cash memorabilia as well as chainsaws and blades.

South First Food Court (right)

Austinites have a great fondness for food trucks, and a visit to the city would not be complete without sampling the wares of one or two. Comprised of half a dozen food trailers, the South First Food Court is just one of many locations that offer a variety of foods for every taste bud.

Maria's Taco X-press (top)

For more than 20 years, Maria's Taco X-press has been one of Austin's favorite go-to Mexican restaurants. It features creative drinks, delicious food, free live music, and supports the local arts community. A larger-than-life statue of owner Maria Corbalan atop the building adds to what makes Austin weird.

Hippie Opera (bottom)

Located along the side of Maria's Taco X-press building, this whimsical hippie opera mural is a popular scenic stop and fits in perfectly with what makes Austin weird. The Taco X-press's Hippie Church gathers Sundays to dance, sing, eat, and enjoy groovy gospel tunes.

Greetings from Austin (top)

The famous *Greetings from Austin* postcard mural is painted on the side of the Roadhouse Relics' store and draws tourists to pose for "wish-you-were-here" memorial photos. Created in 1998 by Todd Sanders, more than twenty years later, the mural remains a south side photo-op attraction.

Franklin Barbecue (bottom)

Backyard BBQ cookouts inspired Aaron Franklin and his wife, Stacy, to open a barbecue trailer in Austin in 2009. Today, Franklin has been acclaimed as one of the most influential pitmasters in the United States and has had the honor of serving Barack Obama, Jimmy Kimmel, and the late Anthony Bourdain.

Stevie Ray Vaughan Memorial

Blues guitarist extraordinaire Stevie Ray Vaughan is immortalized in this larger-than-life statue on Auditorium Shores. Created by Ralph Helmick and installed in 1994, the memorial depicts Rock-and-Roll-Hall-of-Famer Vaughan in his trademark black hat. With deep musical roots in Austin, his legendary songs are often heard in its streets.

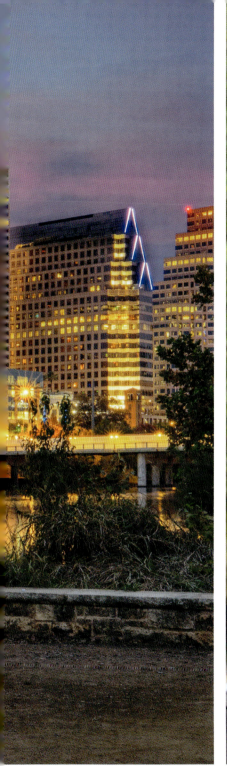

Willie Nelson Statue

With his hippie braids and acoustic guitar, Trigger, this bronze statue of Willie Nelson by artist Clete Shields sits on the corner of 2nd Street, otherwise known as Willie Nelson Boulevard. Although not a native of Austin, Nelson recorded here extensively and often performed in the area.

Paramount Theatre *(above and opposite)*

Paramount Theatre began as a vaudeville house in 1915. Since then, it has presented more than 10,000 artists and screens more than 100 films annually. Originally the "Majestic Theatre," it has hosted Harry Houdini, Katharine Hepburn, President Barack Obama, and Carol Burnett, to name a few.

ZACH Theatre *(left)*

The Zach Theatre, named after Austin native and Academy-Award nominated actor Zachary Scott, is known as the longest-running theatre in Texas. It is the city's best live-theatre venue, hosting more than 500 outstanding performances per year, including musicals, plays, original works, and theatre for youth.

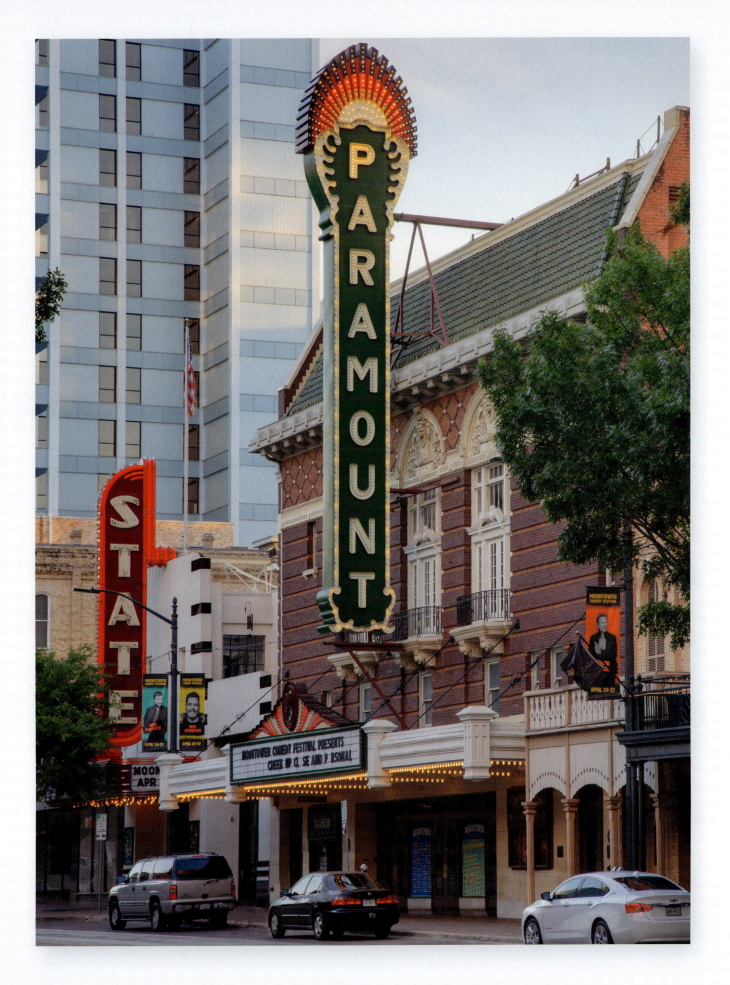

Long Center for the Performing Arts
(top and bottom)

Located on a grassy hilltop overlooking downtown, the Long Center is the entertainment sage for Austin. It features a grand concert hall, adaptable theatre, a concert park, lounges, and educational rooms. With a diverse set of stages and venues, it is a place of constant creativity, indoors and out.

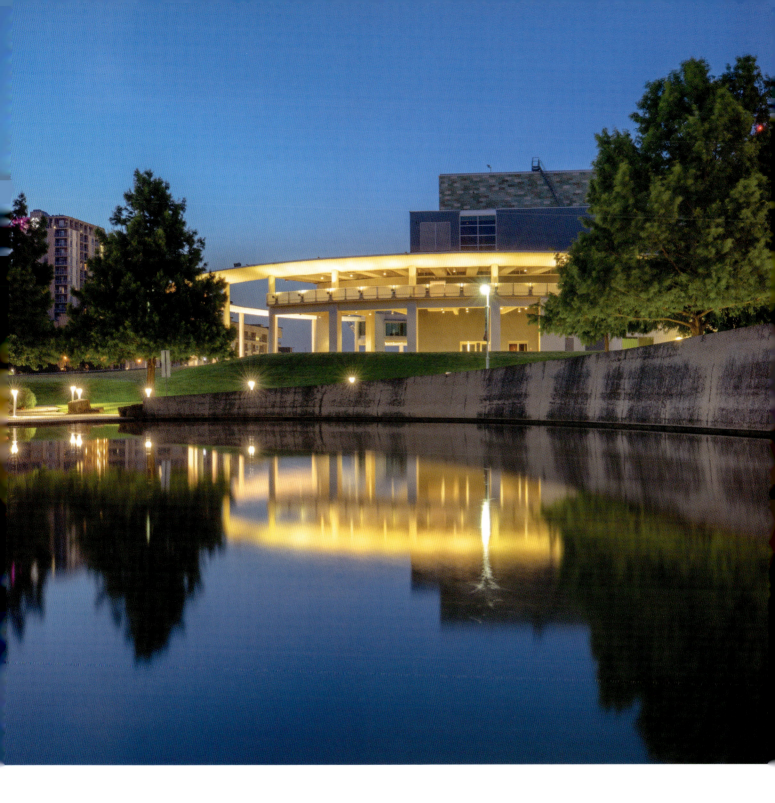

Long Center for the Performing Arts

Constructed in 2008 on the site of Austin's previous performance venue, the Palmer Auditorium, and using 95% recycled material from it, the Long Center's grand white columns and circular ring are a stunning architectural feature. The center is the home of Ballet Austin, Austin Symphony Orchestra, and Austin Lyric Opera.

Skyline at Dawn

Awash in pink and blue hues, Austin's early morning skyline is mirrored in the tranquil surface of the water feature at the Palmer Events Center. Located near the Long Center for the Performing Arts, the center is a multi-purpose venue that provides space for smaller meetings and special events.

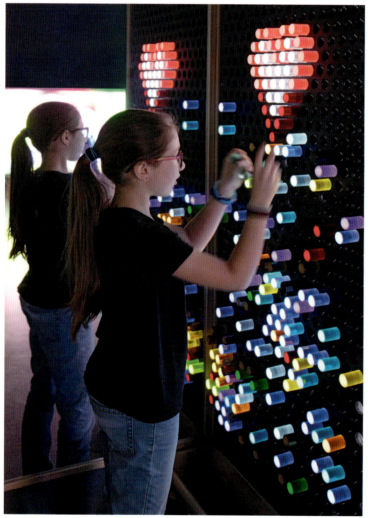

Thinkery *(above and left)*

Helping to create a lifelong passion for creative, critical learning, Thinkery was founded in 1983 as the Austin Children's Museum. Newly opened as Thinkery in 2013 and geared toward children eight months to 11 years, it is where knowledge-centered families come to discover the wonders of science.

Thinkery *(left and right)*

Encouraging interactive learning experiences in science, technology, engineering, and arts and math, Thinkery is Austin's favorite place for kids to play. Its 40,000-square-foot indoor/outdoor center features exhibits: *Light Lab*, *Innovator's Workshop*, *Kitchen Lab*, *Our Backyard*, *Let's Grow*, *Currents*, *Spark Shop*, and *Bloom*.

Cathedral of Junk
(top, bottom, and opposite)

Cathedral of Junk is roughly 60 tons of discarded items that artist Vince Hannemann has carefully and artfully been assembling since 1989. Located on Lareina Drive and open by appointment only, it has been featured in commercials and videos and has been the location for weddings and plays.

ABC Zilker Kite Festival (above)

The ABC Kite Festival in Zilker Park has been fostering creativity in children since 1929. It is one of Austin's most beloved events held on the first Sunday in March and is the longest-running kite festival in the country. Families participate in a kite contest, a fun run, a children's music concert, and more.

Fun on Lady Bird Lake (left and opposite)

Stand-up paddleboarders and kayakers enjoy the calm, spring-fed waters of Lady Bird Lake. Located in the heart of the city and backdropped by Austin's skyline, the lake is home to Zilker Park, Auditorium Shores, and the Ann and Roy Butler Hike-and-Bike Trail. Paddleboards and kayaks are available for rent.

Lady Bird Lake *(above and opposite)*

Lady Bird Lake's water activities include stand-up paddleboarding, canoeing, kayaking, sculling, and riverboat cruising. While swimming is not allowed, it is always filled with water sports enthusiasts. The reservoir was created by the City of Austin in 1960, spans 416 acres, and has a maximum depth of 18 feet.

Aerial over Austin *(top and bottom)*

An aerial view of Austin's skyline captures the city's unique fall colors in November. Reds, greens, and blues coat the edges of Lady Bird Lake. The lake is as wildly beautiful at sunrise as it is in the evening—both perfect times to stroll along the boardwalk and capture its amazing essence.

Austin City Limits

The Austin City Limits Music Festival was founded in 2002 and inspired by the Austin City Limits PBS/KLRU music series. The two-week series, located on the grounds of Zilker Park, includes eight stages and attracts more than 140 bands and 450,000 attendees. The festival supports local artists, food vendors, and nonprofits.

Austin Zoo *(above and left)*

Since 1990, the non-profit Austin Zoo has committed itself to animal rescue, rehabilitation, and education. Children encounter animals from the big cat family, native Texas wildlife, domestic animals, primates, birds, reptiles and amphibians, and more. Fun educational programs are offered to animal lovers of all ages.

Austin Zoo *(above and right)*

The colorful entryway and gift shop of the Austin Zoo welcomes visitors with educational guides, souvenirs, and food for hand-feeding some of the animals. With animals from all over the world that have been rescued from unfortunate circumstances, it has become a popular location for birthday parties and field trips.

The Oasis on Lake Travis *(above)*

The Oasis is a popular spot overlooking Lake Travis where visitors come for delicious food and to watch the sunset from their multiple dining decks. The largest outdoor restaurant in Texas, it offers live music, specialty drinks, a variety of foods, fine wines, and creative desserts.

Lake Travis Harbor *(opposite)*

Lake Travis, a 65-mile-long reservoir on the Colorado River, is the most popular waterway in Central Texas. Just 19 miles from Austin, its 271 miles of shoreline is a popular spot for boating, water skiing, swimming, fishing, and a variety of other water sports.

McKinney Falls State Park
(top and bottom)

A great destination for hiking, camping, and swimming, the McKinney Falls State Park is located just outside of Austin. Named after Thomas McKinney, who owned the area in 1850, it features the ruins of his house, a gristmill, and a horse trainer's cabin. The park has 81 campsites and miles of hiking trails.

McKinney Falls State Park

The slow-moving water of Onion Creek flows past towering cypress trees. "Old Baldy," a 103-foot-tall, 500-year-old bald cypress tree, is one of the oldest bald cypress trees on public land in Texas. Other tree species found in the park include sycamore, pecan, live oak, Ashe juniper, and mesquite.

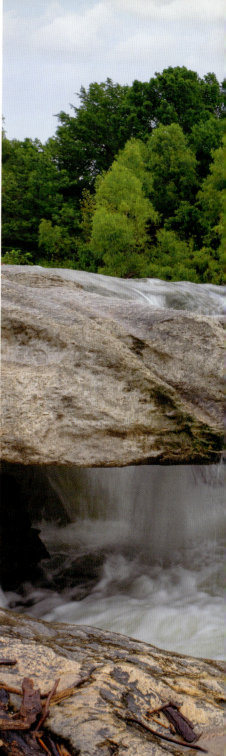

McKinney Falls State Park
Lower Falls *(above and opposite)*

Rushing water from Onion Creek cascades over limestone ledges to the pool at Lower Falls at the McKinney Falls State Park. A series of two waterfalls, an upper and lower, are both deep enough for diving and jumping and offer some of the best swimming in Austin.

Hamilton Pool Preserve
(above and opposite)

Hamilton Pool Preserve Stairs *(left)*

A popular Austin destination, Hamilton Pool Preserve was created when an underground river collapsed. This historic swimming hole is located 23 miles from the city. Hamilton Creek cascades over a limestone cropping to create a 50-foot-tall waterfall surrounded by a grotto laden with moss, maidenhair fern, and cliff swallows.

Hamilton Pool Preserve Stairs *(left)*

Steps lead to the path behind the Hamilton Pool Preserve's waterfall, where water droplets fall from the ceiling. Part of the Balcones Canyonlands Preserve, a 30,428-acre system of endangered species habitat, it provides a haven for a variety of wildlife including endangered golden-cheeked warblers.

Jourdan-Bachman Pioneer Farm

Part of a living history museum, the circa 1850 Scarborough Barn is made of hand-sawn timbers fastened with wooden pegs. The 90-acre Jourdan-Bachman Pioneer Farm transports visitors back to the 1800s with historic-themed areas that tell the story of Texas's past through guided tours or by following a map with historical details.

Sprinkle Corner *(top and bottom)*

Sprinkle Corner, a recreated 1899 rural village, features a town square, exhibits, several houses and buildings, and the General Store where tickets for admission to the farm can be purchased along with old-time candies, books, gifts, and more. Much of the store's décor includes artifacts from early-day stores in Central Texas.

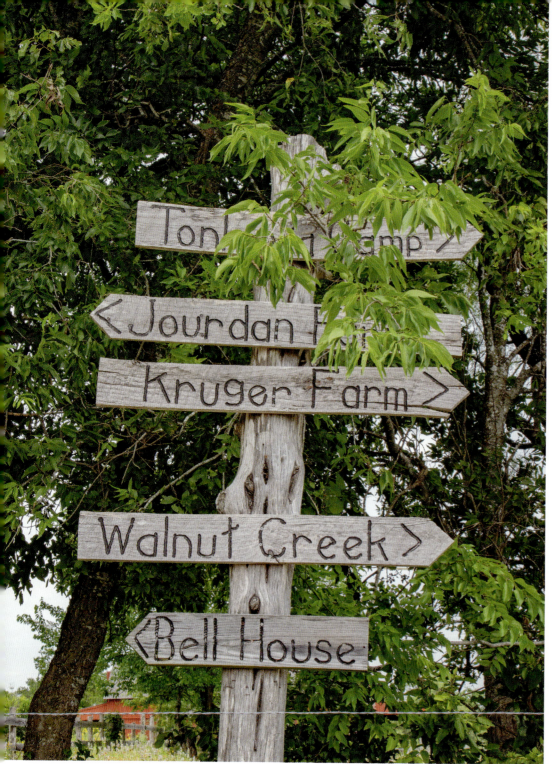

Where to Next?

A whimsical sign helps direct visitors at Jourdan-Bachman Pioneer Farms to its various themed sites. Aside from experiencing life in the 1800s, the farm offers workshops on heritage trades and skills, guided programs for school and community groups, special events, culinary glasses, and more.

Tonkawa Encampment Site

Located along Walnut Creek on an actual Tonkawa campsite from centuries ago, conical tents were made from deer and buffalo skins, similar to this one at the Tonkawa Encampment. Built with a top vent, Tonkawa people were able to lite a fire in its center for cooking and warmth.

Interior Furnishings
(opposite and bottom)

Experience Texas life in the 1800s by stepping inside one of the many homes on the farm. The core of the museum was once the homestead of Frederick and Harriet Jourdan. The farm opened in 1975 and features a German Farm, Texian Farm, Cotton Planter's Farm, one-room cabin, and more.

Fritz Kruger Cabin *(top)*

After immigrating to Texas from Germany in the 1850s, Fritz Kruger constructed this one-room, cedar cabin in 1867, where he and his wife raised 13 children. The parents slept in the cabin while the children slept in the upstairs loft or the barn. Meals were prepared in an outdoor kitchen, and water was fetched from a nearby creek.

360 Bridge

Rob Greebon is a fourth generation Texan who lives in the Texas Hill Country. For twenty years, he's been pursuing landscapes and cityscapes and traveling across Texas and Colorado, seeking out photographic opportunities. He shoots for several magazines, including *Texas Highways, Texas Parks and Wildlife,* and *Outdoor Photographer,* and has been published both locally and nationally. Not far from Austin, Texas, Rob currently resides with his wife and two little girls in the quiet town of Dripping Springs. To learn more about Rob, visit www.imagesfromtexas.com.

Reagan O'Hare, writer, photographer, has fallen in love with the city of Austin. Drawn to the creative spark musicians and artists bring to Austin, her favorite spot is the Pfluger Pedestrian Bridge. The bridge is just a mile from the city's bank of historical and creative hot spots like the Saxon Pub, where you can find her taking photos and serving musicians with bios and positive reviews. O'Hare has written for numerous publications, non-profit organizations, and contributed to musician bios like *Father of a Rock Star,* by Robert Schneider Sr., father of Austin's Bob Schneider. Her tributes to greats like Sting, Willie Nelson, Bob Schneider, Hayes Carll, Jeff Plankenhorn, and Bill Murra can be found at theinvisiblejournalist.wonderwriter.net and www.reaganashleyphotography.com.